FEB 2 0 2013

P9-CDX-732

Pre-Algebra AND Algebra

Ace your Math Test

Rebecca Wingard-Nelson

Enslow Publishers, Inc.
40 Industrial Road
Box 398
Berkeley Heights, NJ 07922
USA

http://www.enslow.com

Library of Congress Cataloging-in-Publication Data
Wingard-Nelson, Rebecca.
   Pre-algebra and algebra / Rebecca Wingard-Nelson.
      p. cm. — (Ace your math test)
   Summary: "Re-inforce in-class algebra and pre-algebra skills such as rational numbers,
absolute values, and problems with inequalities"—Provided by publisher.
   Includes index.
   ISBN 978-0-7660-3782-3
   1. Algebra—Juvenile literature. 2. Numbers, Rational—Juvenile literature. 3. Inequalities
(Mathematics)—Juvenile literature. I. Title.
   QA155.15.W5647 2011
   512—dc22
                                        2010048150

Paperback ISBN 978-1-4644-0009-4
ePUB ISBN 978-1-4645-0458-7
PDF ISBN 978-1-4646-0458-4

Printed in the United States of America

092011 Lake Book Manufacturing, Inc., Melrose Park, IL

10 9 8 7 6 5 4 3 2 1

To Our Readers: We have done our best to make sure all Internet Addresses in this book
were active and appropriate when we went to press. However, the author and the publisher
have no control over and assume no liability for the material available on those Internet sites
or on other Web sites they may link to. Any comments or suggestions can be sent by e-mail
to comments@enslow.com or to the address on the back cover.

♻ Enslow Publishers, Inc., is committed to printing our books on recycled paper. The paper
in every book contains 10% to 30% post-consumer waste (PCW). The cover board on the
outside of each book contains 100% PCW. Our goal is to do our part to help young people
and the environment too!

Illustration Credits: Shutterstock.com

Cover Photos: © iStockphoto.com/Ann Marie Kurtz

CONTENTS

Test-Taking Tips

Be Prepared!

Most of the topics that are found on math tests are taught in the classroom. Paying attention in class, taking good notes, and keeping up with your homework are the best ways to be prepared for tests.

Practice

Use test preparation materials, such as flash cards and timed worksheets, to practice your basic math skills. Take practice tests. They show the kinds of items that will be on the actual test. They can show you what areas you understand, and what areas you need more practice in.

Test Day!

The Night Before

Relax. Eat a good meal. Go to bed early enough to get a good night's sleep. Don't cram on new material! Review the material you know is going to be on the test.

Get what you need ready. Sharpen your pencils, set out things like erasers, a calculator, and any extra materials, like books, protractors, tissues, or cough drops.

The Big Day

Get up early enough to eat breakfast and not have to hurry. Wear something that is comfortable and makes you feel good. Listen to your favorite music.

Get to school and class on time. Stay calm. Stay positive.

Test Time!

Before you begin, take a deep breath. Focus on the test, not the people or things around you. Remind yourself to do your best and not to worry about what you do not know.

Work through the entire test, but don't spend too much time on any one problem. Don't rush, but move quickly, first answering all of the questions you can do easily. Go back a second time and answer the questions that take more time.

Read each question completely. Read all the answer choices. Eliminate answers that are obviously wrong. Read word problems carefully, and decide what the problem is asking.

Check each answer to make sure it is reasonable. Estimate numbers to see if your answer makes sense.

Concentrate on the test. Stay focused. If your attention starts to wander, take a short break. Breathe. Relax. Refocus. Don't get upset if you can't answer a question. Mark it, then come back to it later.

When you finish, look back over the entire test. Are all of the questions answered? Check as many problems as you can. Look at your calculations and make sure you have the same answer on the blank as you do on your worksheet.

Let's Go!

Three common types of test problems are covered in this book: Multiple Choice, Show Your Work, and Explain Your Answer. Tips on how to solve each, as well as common errors to avoid, are also presented. Knowing what to expect on a test and what is expected of you will have you ready to ace every math test you take.

1. Integers

Numbers

There are different types of numbers that are used to show different values.

Definitions

whole numbers: The numbers 0, 1, 2, 3, 4, 5, . . .

counting numbers: The whole numbers except for 0.

natural numbers: Natural numbers are defined in two ways, either the set of whole numbers, or the set of counting numbers.

integers: Whole numbers and their opposites.

Is the number ⁻2 a whole number?

Step 1: Find the definition of a whole number. Whole numbers are the numbers that begin at zero and go up by intervals of one. The lowest whole number is zero. The number ⁻2 is a negative number. It is less than zero.

No, ⁻2 is not a whole number.

TEST TIME: Explain Your Answer

Is the number 7 a whole number, counting number, or integer? Explain.

Solution: The only whole number that is not a counting number is zero. Since 7 is not zero, it is a whole number and a counting number. Integers include the set of all whole numbers. Since 7 is a whole number, it is also an integer.

The number 7 is a whole number, a counting number, and an integer.

Test-Taking Hint

Some problems ask a question and ask you to explain your answer. Others just ask for an answer. Your score may be based on a correct response as well as how clearly you explain your reasoning.

Integers

The set of integers includes positive integers, negative integers, and zero. Opposite integers are the same distance from zero on the number line.

What integer is the opposite of ⁻5?

Step 1: Opposite integers are the same distance from zero on the number line, but are on opposite sides. The integer is five units left of zero. Find the integer that is five units right of zero.

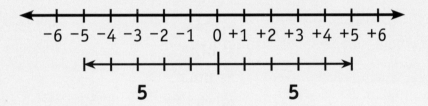

The opposite of ⁻5 is ⁺5.

Test-Taking Hint

Multiple choice problems give you a list of solutions. Other kinds of problems ask you to provide the solution. Problems that ask you to provide the solution should be answered clearly and in complete sentences.

TEST TIME: Multiple Choice

Which number line illustrates the positive integer 4?

a.

-8 -7 -6 -5 -4 -3 -2 -1 0

b.

-5 -4 -3 -2 -1 0 1 2 3

c.

-3 -2 -1 0 1 2 3 4 5

d.

-3 -2 -1 0 1 2 3 4 5

Positive integers are greater than zero. On a number line, the positive integers are to the right of the zero. Negative integers are to the left of the zero. Since this problem asks for the positive integer, the answer will be to the right of the zero on the number line. The only answer that is to the right of the zero is answer c. Make sure it shows the positive integer 4.

Solution: The correct answer is c.

2. Rational Numbers

Real Numbers

The set of real numbers is made up of two types of numbers: rational numbers and irrational numbers.

Definitions

rational numbers: Numbers that can be written as a ratio, or fraction. For example, 1/4 is a rational number. All integers are rational numbers because they can be written as fractions. $5 = 5/1$

irrational numbers: Numbers that cannot be written as a ratio. Decimal numbers that do not end and do not repeat are irrational numbers. The square root of 3 and the number represented by π are irrational numbers.

Is ⁻0.5 a rational number or an irrational number?

Step 1: Rational numbers can be either positive or negative. Look at the number without looking at the sign.

0.5

Step 2: Can you write 0.5 as a fraction? Yes. Decimal numbers are written as fractions by writing the decimal part of the number in the numerator and the place value of the last digit in the decimal part as the denominator. The digit 5 is in the tenths place, so use ten as the denominator. Reduce the fraction to lowest terms.

$$5/10 = 1/2$$

Step 3: Put the original sign (negative) on the fraction.

$$-1/2$$

The number ⁻0.5 can be written as the negative fraction −1/2. Any number that can be written as a fraction is a rational number.

−0.5 is a rational number.

TEST TIME: Show Your Work

Make a diagram that shows how integers and whole, counting, rational, irrational, and real numbers are related.

You must know the relationships between the sets of numbers in order to draw this diagram. Let's begin by comparing the first three sets of numbers in the problem: integers, whole numbers, and counting numbers.

Integers are the set of whole numbers AND their opposites. This means that all whole numbers are integers, but not all integers are whole numbers. This can be drawn by showing a larger circle to represent the set of integers and a smaller circle inside the integer circle to represent the set of whole numbers.

Counting numbers are part of the set of whole numbers, but do not include zero. Draw another circle or oval inside the set of whole numbers for the counting numbers.

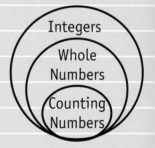

The next set of numbers listed is rational numbers. Rational numbers include all integers, but also include numbers that are NOT integers, like fractions and decimals. Use a larger space for rational numbers that includes the set of integers. Since all integers are rational

TEST TIME, CONTINUED

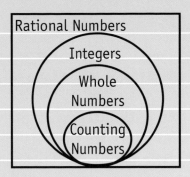

numbers, make sure the entire
integer circle is inside the set
of rational numbers.
Let's use a square.

The remaining two sets of numbers are irrational and real numbers.
Rational and irrational numbers do not overlap. Together, they make
up the entire set of real numbers. Draw a second square for irrational
numbers. Put it directly against the rational numbers, but not
overlapping. The set of real numbers includes both of these sets
and nothing else.

Solution:

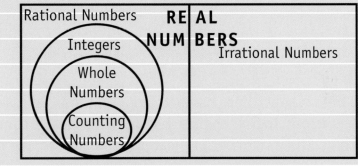

Test-Taking Hint
Not all of the questions on a math test need computations.
Know math definitions and know the reasons behind the math.

3. Comparing Numbers

Positives and Negatives

As with integers, there are positive and negative rational numbers. You can use a number line to understand how rational numbers are related to each other.

Which number is greater, ⁻1.5 or ⁻3?

Step 1: One way to compare numbers is to look at the numbers on a number line.

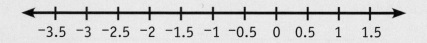

Find the numbers you are comparing on the number line.

Step 2: On a number line, numbers are greater as you move right. This means the numbers are in least to greatest order from left to right. Which number is greater (or farther to the right)?

⁻1.5 is greater than ⁻3.

TEST TIME: Explain Your Answer

The temperature Tuesday was ⁻4°F.
The temperature Wednesday was 2°F.
Reagan said it was colder Wednesday because 2 is less than 4.
Is she correct? Explain.

This problem asks if Reagan is correct. It also asks for an explanation. Be sure to include all of the required answers.

Solution: Reagan is not correct. She is correct in knowing that a lower temperature is colder than a higher temperature. However, she did not understand that the temperature on Tuesday was a negative number, and negative numbers always have a lower value than positive numbers. It would have helped Reagan if she had looked at a thermometer to compare the temperatures. ⁻4°F is lower on the thermometer and therefore colder than 2°F.

⁻4 is less than 2, so Tuesday was colder than Wednesday.

Definitions

equal sign (=): The two numbers or expressions on opposites sides of this sign have the same value.

less than sign (<): The number or expression on the left has a value that is less than the number or expression on the right.

greater than sign (>): The number or expression on the left has a value that is greater than the number or expression on the right.

Use the symbols <, >, or = to compare 3/4 and 1/2.

Step 1: Fractions are one type of rational number. To compare fractions with different denominators, first rewrite them so they have the same denominator.

To change a denominator of 2 to a denominator of 4, multiply the numerator and denominator by 2.

$$\frac{1}{2} = \frac{1 \times 2}{2 \times 2} = \frac{2}{4}$$

Step 2: Compare the like fractions 3/4 and 2/4 by comparing the numerators.

$3 > 2$, so $3/4 > 2/4$ $\qquad\qquad$ $3/4 > 1/2$

Which set puts the numbers
3, ⁻6, ⁻4, and 0 in order from least to greatest?

a. 0, 3, ⁻4, ⁻6
b. ⁻4, ⁻6, 0, 3
c. ⁻6, ⁻4, 0, 3
d. 3, ⁻4, ⁻6, 0

You can use what you know about positive and negative numbers. Negative numbers are always less than positive numbers. Zero is the dividing point between positive and negative numbers. Answers a and d both have positive numbers listed before negative, so they are not the correct answers. A negative number has a lesser value when the number part is "bigger." ⁻6 has a "bigger" number part than ⁻4, so it has a lesser value and should be listed first.

Solution: Answer c is the correct answer.

Test-Taking Hint
Some multiple choice questions can be solved by eliminating choices that are obviously incorrect.

4. Absolute Value

Positive Numbers

What is the value of |6|?

Step 1: The absolute value of 6 is the distance from zero to 6 on the number line. You can use a number line and count the number of units, or you can use what you know about numbers. The number 6 is a distance of 6 units from zero on the number line.

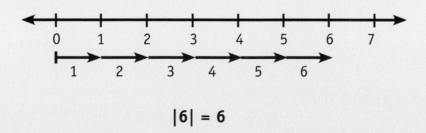

$$|6| = 6$$

TEST TIME: Show Your Work

What is the absolute value of ⁻2.5?

You can find the distance from zero to −2.5 on the number line. Remember, absolute value is always a positive value.

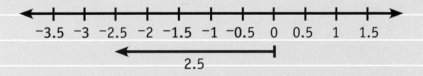

Solution: The distance from 0 to −2.5 is 2.5 units.

|⁻2.5| = 2.5

Extras

For every positive number, the absolute value is the same as the number.

For every negative number, the absolute value is the same as the number without the negative sign.

Absolute Value and Computations

Find the difference.

$$|^-6| - |2|$$

Step 1: For this problem, you must find the absolute value of each number before you subtract.

$$|^-6| = 6 \qquad |2| = 2$$

Step 2: Rewrite the problem using the absolute values.

$$6 - 2$$

Step 3: Subtract.

$$6 - 2 = 4$$

$$|^-6| - |2| = 4$$

Test-Taking Hint

Some multiple choice problems offer an answer choice all of the above. Make sure you check all of these possible choices before you select your answer.

TEST TIME: Multiple Choice

Which of the following expressions has a value of 7?

> a. $|-4| + |3|$
> b. $|16 - 9|$
> c. $|5 + 2|$
> d. All of the above

Find the value of each expression.
When the operation is NOT inside the absolute value sign, as in answer a, find the absolute values first, then add or subtract.

> a. $|-4| + |3| = 4 + 3 = 7$

When the operation is inside the absolute value sign, as in answers b and c, do the math first, then find the absolute value.

> b. $|16 - 9| = |7| = 7$
> c. $|5 + 2| = |7| = 7$

The expressions for answers a, b, and c all have a value of 7.

Solution: Answer d is correct.

5. Addition: Like Signs

Like Integers

Integers that have the same sign (positive or negative) are called like integers.

What is the sum of $^+5 + {}^+3$?

Step 1: Positive integers are normally written without the positive sign. Write the problem without the positive signs.

$$5 + 3$$

Step 2: Add.

$$5 + 3 = 8$$

Step 3: Since the problem uses the positive sign, put the sign in the answer.

$$^+5 + {}^+3 = {}^+8$$

Definitions

addends: The numbers that are added in an addition problem.

sum: The answer to an addition problem.

Negative Numbers

Add $^-4 + {}^-6$.

Step 1: When both integers have the same sign, you can add the absolute values of the integers.

$$|{}^-4| + |{}^-6| = 4 + 6 = 10$$

Step 2: Put the negative signs back in. The addends are negative, so the sum is also negative.

$$^-4 + {}^-6 = {}^-10$$

TEST TIME: Show Your Work

Trevor ran a football for a 3-yard gain. Then he ran a second play for a 6-yard gain. What was the overall gain?

A gain is a positive number. Add the two gains.
$^+3 + {}^+6 = {}^+9$
Write the answer in a complete sentence.

Solution: There was an overall gain of 9 yards.

Rational Numbers

Rational numbers with the same signs are added in the same way as integers with the same signs. Add the absolute values. The sum has the same sign as the addends.

Add $^+1.5 + {}^+2.8$.

Step 1: Add the absolute values. With decimal numbers it is often easier to write the numbers in a column and line up the decimal points.

$$|^+1.5| + |^+2.8| = \quad \begin{array}{r} 1.5 \\ + \ 2.8 \\ \hline 4.3 \end{array}$$

Step 2: Since the problem uses positive signs, put the signs in the answer.

$$^+1.5 + {}^+2.8 = {}^+4.3$$

Test-Taking Hint

An answer in a multiple choice problem might look correct if you look too quickly. Often the wrong answers listed are ones you would find if you made a common error.

TEST TIME: Multiple Choice

Marcia withdrew $26.42 from her checking account using a debit card. She withdrew another $10.00 for parking. What number represents the change in her account balance for the day?

> a. $36.42
> b. $16.42
> c. −$16.42
> (d.) −$36.42

When money is withdrawn from an account, it can be represented by a negative number. The first withdrawal can be represented by −$26.42, and the second by −$10.00. To find the total change in the account balance, add the withdrawals for the day.

$|^-\$26.42| + |^-\$10.00| = \$26.42 + \$10.00 = \$36.42$
$^-\$26.42 + {}^-\$10.00 = {}^-\$36.42$

Be careful. Answer a looks correct if you don't include the negative sign.

Solution: Answer d is correct.

6. Addition: Unlike Signs

Unlike Integers

Integers that have different signs (positive or negative) are called unlike integers.

Add ⁺4 and ⁻8.

Step 1: Use a number line to help you understand addition of unlike integers. Begin on the number line at the first addend, ⁺4.

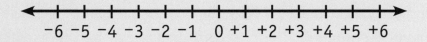

Step 2: To add a positive value on a number line, move right. To add a negative value on a number line, move left. Move left 8 units.

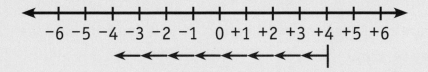

Step 3: You end at ⁻4.

$$^{+}4 + {^{-}8} = {^{-}4}$$

TEST TIME: Multiple Choice

What is the sum of −3 + +2?

a. −5
(b.) −1
c. +1
d. +5

The addends in this problem have different signs. You can use mental reasoning to understand that the negative integer is one unit farther from zero than the positive integer. That means the sum or combination will be one negative unit.

Solution: Answer b is correct.

You can check the answer to this problem using a number line. Begin at the first addend, ⁻3. To add a positive 2, move right 2 units.

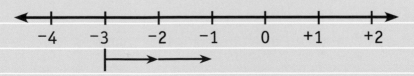

TEST TIME: Show Your Work

In a beanbag game, a team gains points for tossing a beanbag into a hole. They lose points when a beanbag goes into the other team's hole. In one round, the red team gained 6 points and lost 4 points. Write an equation and solve it to find the gain or loss for that round.

A positive integer can be used to represent gains. A negative integer can be used to represent losses. Write an equation that adds the total gains and losses.

$$+6 + {}^-4 = \underline{}$$

Unlike integers can be added by finding the difference of their absolute values. Subtract the smaller absolute value from the larger absolute value.

$$|{+}6| - |{}^-4| = 6 - 4 = 2$$

The final answer has the same sign as the integer with the greater absolute value. Since 6 > 4, the answer is positive.

Solution: $+6 + {}^-4 = +2$

The red team had a gain of 2 points for that round.

Rational Numbers

Rational numbers that have different signs are added in the same way as integers.

Add $^-7/10$ and $^+3/10$.

Step 1: Unlike rationals are added by first finding the difference between their absolute values.

$$|^-7/10| - |^+3/10| = 7/10 - 3/10$$

Step 2: To subtract like fractions, subtract only the numerators and keep the same denominator.

$$7/10 - 3/10 = 4/10$$

Step 3: Reduce to lowest terms.

$$4/10 = 2/5$$

Step 4: The sum has the same sign as the addend with the greater absolute value.

$$7/10 > 3/10$$

$$^-7/10 + {}^+3/10 = {}^-2/5$$

7. Subtraction

Inverse Operations

Addition and subtraction are inverse operations. They do the inverse, or opposite, of each other. You can subtract a number by adding the opposite number.

Subtract $^+2 - {}^-10$.

Step 1: To subtract integers, add the opposite. Write the first number.

$$^+2$$

Step 2: Change the subtraction symbol to an addition symbol.

$$^+2 +$$

Step 3: Write the opposite of the second number.

$$^+2 + {}^+10$$

Step 4: Add. $\qquad ^+2 + {}^+10 = {}^+12$

$$^+2 - {}^-10 = {}^+12$$

> ## Test-Taking Hint
> Watch for clue words in word problems that tell you what operation is being performed.

TEST TIME: Show Your Work

The record high temperature in a city is 96°F. The record low in the same city is ⁻8°F. What is the variation in temperature between the record high and record low?

The word *variation* means difference, so this is a subtraction problem. You can subtract the temperatures by adding the opposite.

Solution:

If you subtract the negative from the positive you get:

$$+96 - {}^{-}8 = +96 + +8 = +104$$

If you subtract the positive from the negative you get:

$$^{-}8 - +96 = {}^{-}8 + {}^{-}96 = {}^{-}104$$

The question is asked in a way that you should use a positive answer.

The record high and low temperatures vary by 104°F.

Subtracting Rationals

Subtract $^-2.6 - ^-8.9$.

Step 1: Subtract rationals by adding the opposite. Write the first number, change the subtraction symbol to addition, then write the opposite of the second number.

$$^-2.6 + {}^+8.9$$

Step 2: Add. Remember, to add numbers with different signs, you need to find the difference of the absolute values.

$$|^+8.9| - |^-2.6| = 6.3$$

Keep the sign of the addend with the greater absolute value.

$$8.9 > 2.6$$

$$^-2.6 - {}^-8.9 = {}^+6.3$$

TEST TIME: Explain Your Answer

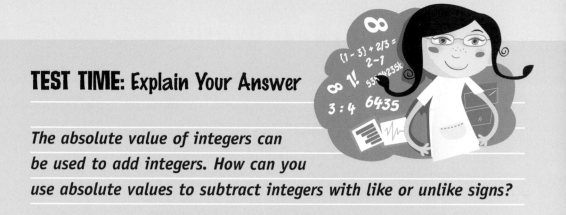

The absolute value of integers can be used to add integers. How can you use absolute values to subtract integers with like or unlike signs?

Solution: To subtract integers with like signs, rewrite the problem as addition. $+2 - +5 = +2 + -5$

Subtract the lesser absolute value from the greater absolute value.

$$|-5| - |+2| = 5 - 2 = 3$$

Keep the sign of the number with the greater absolute value.

$$5 > 2, \text{ so } +2 + -5 = -3 \text{ and } +2 - +5 = -3$$

To subtract integers with unlike signs, rewrite the problem as addition.

$$-2 - +3 = -2 + -3$$

To use absolute value to solve these, you can add the absolute values of the integers, then keep the sign of the first number.

$$|-2| + |-3| = 2 + 3 = 5$$

The first number is negative, so $-2 - +3 = -5$

So, for subtraction of like integers, add the opposite, subtract the absolute values, and take the sign of the greater absolute value.

For subtraction of unlike integers, add the opposite, add the absolute values, and take the sign of the first number.

8. Addition Properties

The Commutative Property

Changing the order of the addends in an addition problem does not change the sum.

Show that +3 + −2 has the same value as −2 + +3.

Step 1: Find the value of the first expression. Add the integers by finding the difference of their absolute values.

$$+3 + {}^-2$$
$$|{}^+3| - |{}^-2| = 3 - 2 = 1, 3 > 2, \text{ so}$$

$$+3 + {}^-2 = {}^+1$$

Step 2: Find the value of the second expression. Add the integers by finding the difference of their absolute values. Subtract the smaller absolute value from the larger.

$$-2 + {}^+3$$
$$|{}^+3| - |{}^-2| = 3 - 2 = 1, 3 > 2, \text{ so}$$

$$-2 + {}^+3 = {}^+1$$

Step 3: Compare the sums.

$$+3 + {}^-2 = {}^+1 \text{ and } {}^-2 + {}^+3 = {}^+1$$

The order of the addends is changed, but the sums are the same.

TEST TIME: Multiple Choice

Kevin is on the wrestling team and keeps close track of his weight. In October, Kevin gained 6.2 pounds. In November, he lost 2.1 pounds, and in December, he lost another 3.1 pounds. What is Kevin's total gain or loss for the three months?

(a.) 1.0-pound gain

b. 1.0-pound loss

c. 5.2-pound loss

d. 7.2-pound gain

Gains are positive values and losses are negative values. Add the value for each month. $+6.2 + {}^-2.1 + {}^-3.1$

The Associative Property says that you can change the grouping of how you add numbers. Instead of adding the first two numbers first, add the last two numbers first. This combines the negative values first. Use parentheses to show the addition order.

$$+6.2 + (^-2.1 + {}^-3.1) = +6.2 + {}^-5.2 = +1$$

A positive value is a gain, so the total for the three months is a one-pound gain.

Solution: Answer a is correct.

The Zero Property

Add ⁻*23.9* + *0.*

Step 1: Zero is a neutral. It is neither positive nor negative. Add the values as you do for numbers with different signs. Find the difference of the absolute values.

$$|{}^-23.9| - |0| = 23.9 - 0 = 23.9$$

Adding a zero to any number does not change the value of the number.

Test-Taking Hint

Knowing the properties can make solving addition problems easier. Be careful to only apply the addition properties to addition; they are NOT all true for subtraction.

TEST TIME: Multiple Choice

What is the sum of ⁻3 + ⁺3?

      a. ⁻6
      b. ⁻3
      ⓒ 0
      d. ⁺6

The addends in this problem are opposite integers.
The Inverse Property says that when you add numbers
that are opposites, the sum is zero.

Solution: Answer c is correct.

You can check the answer to this problem using a number line.
Begin at the first addend, ⁻3. To add a positive 3, move right
3 units.

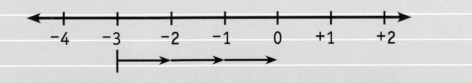

9. Multiplication

Definitions

factors: The numbers that are multiplied in a multiplication problem.

product: The answer to a multiplication problem.

Multiplying Positives and Negatives

Multiplication of values with positive and negative signs is similar to other multiplication. The absolute value of the answer, or product, is the same. The only difference is knowing if the product is positive or negative.

Multiply $+3 \times +2$ and -3×-2.

Step 1: Multiply the integers without the signs.

$$3 \times 2 = 6$$

Step 2: Place the signs in the product. When two factors both have the same sign (two positives or two negatives), the product is positive.

$$+3 \times +2 = +6 \qquad -3 \times -2 = +6$$

TEST TIME: Show Your Work

Trevor's parking pass has a $20 balance. Each day there is a $3 charge. After 6 days, what is the new balance on the pass?

There is a positive balance of $20 on the pass. Each day for 6 days there is a charge of $3. A charge is a negative amount.
One way to solve this problem is to break it into two parts.
First find the total of the charges, then find the new balance.

The total charges are found by multiplying a positive number of days by a negative dollar value. A negative multiplied by a positive is a negative.

Solution: The total charges are 6 days times −$3.
$$6 \times -\$3 = -\$18$$

Add the balance and the total charges.
$$\$20 + -\$18 = \$2$$

The new balance on Trevor's parking pass is $2.

Multiplication of Rationals

Multiply −12 and $\frac{1}{4}$.

Step 1: Multiply without using the signs. A whole number and a fraction are multiplied by writing the whole number as an improper fraction with a denominator of 1.

$$\frac{12}{1} \times \frac{1}{4}$$

Step 2: Simplify by dividing the numerator of one fraction and the denominator of the other by a common factor. In this problem, you can divide 12 by 4, and 4 by 4.

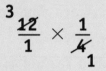

Step 3: Multiply the numerators and multiply the denominators.

$$\frac{3}{1} \times \frac{1}{1} = \frac{3 \times 1}{1 \times 1} = \frac{3}{1} = 3$$

Step 4: Place the sign in the product. One factor is negative, and one is positive. The product is negative.

$$-12 \times \frac{1}{4} = {}^{-}3$$

Multiplication Rules

Like signs: When two factors have the same sign, the product is positive. $(+ \times + = + \; ; \; - \times - = +)$

Unlike signs: When two factors have different signs, the product is negative. $(+ \times - = - \; ; \; - \times + = -)$

TEST TIME: Multiple Choice

The temperature of the water coming out of a shower head decreased by 1.6°F per minute of shower time. If Sam took a 4 minute shower, what number best represents the change in temperature of the water?

- (a.) −6.4°F
- b. −5.4°F
- c. 5.4°F
- d. 6.4°F

Multiply the temperature change per minute by the number of minutes. The temperature of the water is decreasing, or a negative change. The number of minutes is a positive value. The signs of the factors are different, so the product is negative.

$+4 \times -1.6 = -6.4$

Solution: Answer a is correct.

10. Division

Division Rules

Like signs: The quotient of two numbers with the same sign is positive. ($+ \div + = +$; $- \div - = +$)

Unlike signs: The quotient of two numbers with different signs is negative. ($+ \div - = -$; $- \div + = -$)

Dividing Integers

Integers are divided in the same way as whole numbers.

Divide $-20 \div 5$.

Step 1: Divide the integers without using the signs.

$$20 \div 5 = 4$$

Step 2: Place the sign. The signs are unlike, so the quotient, or answer, is negative.

$$-20 \div 5 = -4$$

Definitions

dividend: The number being divided in a division problem.

divisor: The number being divided by in a division problem.

quotient: The answer to a division problem.

$$\text{dividend} \div \text{divisor} = \text{quotient}$$

TEST TIME: Multiple Choice

What is the quotient of $-324 \div -6$?

        a. -54

        b. $+54$

        c. -56

        d. $+56$

Eliminate answers a and c quickly by looking at the signs.
The signs in the problem are like, so the quotient is positive.
Divide without using the signs.

$$324 \div 6 = 54$$

Solution: The correct answer is b.

Check your answer using multiplication.

$$+54 \times -6 = -324$$

Test-Taking Hint

Check your answers whenever you have extra time.
Simple math errors are easy to make when you are
reading and answering questions quickly.

TEST TIME: Show Your Work

Find the quotient of ⁻108.36 ÷ 8.4.

Divide without using the signs. Use long division to find the quotient. To divide a decimal by a decimal, first move the decimal point in the divisor and dividend the same number of places to make the divisor a whole number.

Solution: 108.36 ÷ 8.4   8.4)‾1‾0‾8‾.‾3‾6‾ = 84)‾1‾0‾8‾3‾.‾6‾

$$
\begin{array}{r}
12.9 \\
84\,\overline{)1083.6} \\
-\,84 \\
\hline
243 \\
-\,168 \\
\hline
756 \\
-\,756 \\
\hline
0
\end{array}
$$

The signs are unlike, so ⁻108.36 ÷ 8.4 = ⁻12.9

Test-Taking Hint

A calculator is a useful tool when doing long division. It can be used to find the quotient or it can be used to check your calculations.

Fractions

Fractions are divided by multiplying by the reciprocal.

Divide $6 \div \frac{-2}{3}$.

Step 1: Divide without using the signs. Write the whole number as an improper fraction.

$$\frac{6}{1} \div \frac{2}{3}$$

Step 2: Rewrite the problem using a multiplication sign and the reciprocal.

$$\frac{6}{1} \times \frac{3}{2}$$

Step 3: Simplify.

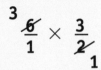

Step 4: Multiply.

$$\frac{3}{1} \times \frac{3}{1} = \frac{3 \times 3}{1 \times 1} = \frac{9}{1}$$

Step 5: The signs are unlike, so the quotient is negative.

$$6 \div \frac{-2}{3} = -9$$

11. Multiplication Properties

The Associative Property

The Associative Property says that when you have more than two factors, you can change the grouping without changing the product.

Does ($^-3 \times 5$) $\times$ 2 have the same product as $^-3 \times$ (5 $\times$ 2)?

Step 1: Multiply ($^-3 \times 5$) $\times$ 2. Multiply inside the parentheses first.

$$(^-3 \times 5) \times 2 = (^-15) \times 2 = {}^-30$$

Step 2: Multiply $^-3 \times$ (5 $\times$ 2). Multiply inside the parentheses first.

$$^-3 \times (5 \times 2) = {}^-3 \times (10) = {}^-30$$

Step 3: Compare the products.

$$(^-3 \times 5) \times 2 = {}^-30 \text{ and } {}^-3 \times (5 \times 2) = {}^-30$$

Yes, ($^-3 \times 5$) $\times$ 2 and $^-3 \times$ (5 $\times$ 2) have the same product, $^-30$.

The only difference between these two multiplication expressions is the order in which the factors are multiplied.

TEST TIME: Multiple Choice

Which of the following illustrates the Commutative Property?

    a. $^-6 \times (2 \times {}^-4) = {}^-6 \times (2 \times {}^-4)$

    b. $2 \times {}^-45 = {}^-45 \times 2$

    c. $1 \times {}^-16 = {}^-16$

    d. $^-2/3 \times {}^-3/2 = 1$

The Commutative Property says changing the order of the factors does not change the product. Answers a and b show how factors can be moved or grouped and have the same value. Answer a keeps the same order, but groups the factors differently. Answer b changes the order of the factors.

Solution: The correct answer is b.

Test-Taking Hint

When a question is taking an especially long time, or has you stumped, leave the question and go on. Come back later if you have time. Another question may give you a clue that can help you solve the problem.

TEST TIME: Explain Your Answer

Show more than one way to solve
⁻6 × (9 + 5). Explain your work.

The Distributive Property can be used when one of the factors in a multiplication problem is written as a sum. You can find the sum first, then multiply. Or you can multiply by each addend separately, then add the products. The answer is the same.

Solution: You can add inside the parentheses first, then multiply.

$$^-6 \times (9 + 5) = {}^-6 \times (14) = {}^-84$$

You can distribute the ⁻6 and multiply, then add the products.

$$^-6 \times (9 + 5) = ({}^-6 \times 9) + ({}^-6 \times 5) = ({}^-54) + ({}^-30) = {}^-84$$

Both methods give an answer of ⁻84.

Other Properties

Name and explain the property illustrated by each of the following equations.

a. 0 × 5 = 0

This equation illustrates the Zero Property. When you multiply any number and zero, the product is always zero.

b. 18 × 1 = 18

This equation illustrates the Identity Property. When you multiply one and any number, the product is always that other number.

c. 4/5 × 5/4 = 1

This equation illustrates the Inverse Property. When you multiply any number and its inverse, the product is always one. An inverse of a rational number is also called a reciprocal.

Definition

inverse of a number: A number that can be multiplied by the original number to result in a product of one.

You can find the inverse of a rational number by writing the number as a fraction, then switching the numerator and denominator.

For example, the inverse of 4, or 4/1, is 1/4.

12. Variables and Expressions

Definitions

expression: A mathematical phrase that combines numbers, variables, and operators to represent a value.

constant: A number in an expression is called a constant because its value does not change.

variable: A value in an expression that is either not known or can change. Variables are usually letters.

Numeric Expressions

Numeric expressions do not use variables, only numbers and operators like + or ÷.

Write a numeric expression that matches this situation: Dana bought a package of ten cookies and ate six of them.

Step 1: Decide what happens in the situation. Dana started with ten cookies, then ate six. So, some of the cookies went away. This is a subtraction situation. Write ten cookies minus six cookies using numbers and operators.

ten cookies minus six cookies

$$10 - 6$$

TEST TIME: Show Your Work

Evaluate the expression −*60* × *8.*

Evaluate means "find the value of." To evaluate a numeric expression, do the operations to find a single number.

You can use mental math and basic multiplication facts to evaluate this expression.

Solution: $6 \times 8 = 48$, so $60 \times 8 = 480$

$$^{-}60 \times 8 = {}^{-}480$$

Test-Taking Hint

When you don't feel confident about an answer, and have time, try solving it a different way. That way, you are less likely to make the same mistake twice.

Algebraic Expressions

Algebraic expressions use variables, usually letters, to represent unknown numbers, or numbers that change.

Each month Yoki deposits exactly $125 into his savings account. Write an expression for the total amount of money Yoki has deposited into his savings account.

Step 1: The number of months Yoki has deposited money into his account is not known. Choose a variable to represent the number of months. You can use the first letter of a word as a variable to help you remember what a variable stands for.

Let m = number of months

Step 2: Each month Yoki deposits the same amount. The total amount is found by multiplying the amount per month by the number of months.

amount per month times number of months

Step 3: Replace the words with numbers, operations symbols, and variables.

$125 \times m$

In algebra, the symbol for multiplication can easily be confused for the letter x. When there is no symbol between parts of an expression, multiplication is understood. Write this expression without the multiplication symbol.

$125m$

TEST TIME: Multiple Choice

Evaluate the expression 8x for x = 20.

      a. 8
      b. 20
      c. 160
      d. 208

Algebraic expressions are evaluated by replacing the variable with the value given in the problem. The expression 8x means to multiply 8 by the given value of x, 20.

$$8 \times 20 = 160$$

Solution: The correct answer is c.

Test-Taking Hint

Work at your own pace. Don't worry about how fast anyone else is taking the same test.

13. Order of Operations

Definition

order of operations: A set of rules that tells what operations are performed first. The order of operations is operations inside Parentheses first, Exponents, Multiplication and Division, and Addition and Subtraction. When operations have the same rank, perform them from left to right.

Simplify Expressions

Simplify the expression $2 + 8(4 - 1)$.

Step 1: For numeric expressions, simplify means the same as evaluate. Follow the order of operations to get to a single number. Are there are operations inside parentheses? Yes. Do those operations first.

$$2 + 8(4 - 1) = 2 + 8(3)$$

Step 2: Are there any exponents? No.
Is there any multiplication or division? Yes. Do those next.

$$2 + 8(3) = 2 + 24$$

Step 3: Is there any addition or subtraction? Yes. Do these last.

$$2 + 24 = 26$$

$$\text{So, } 2 + 8(4 - 1) = 26$$

What expression has the same value as 12 − 8 ÷ 2?

> a. $4 \div 2$
> (b.) $2 + 3 \times 2$
> c. $8 - 10 \div 5$
> d. $8 - 8 \div 2$

Find the value of the expression in the problem.

$12 - 8 \div 2 = 12 - 4 = 8$

Find the value for each expression in the answers.

a. $4 \div 2 = 2$

b. $2 + 3 \times 2 = 2 + 6 = 8$

c. $8 - 10 \div 5 = 8 - 2 = 6$

d. $8 - 8 \div 2 = 8 - 4 = 4$

Solution: The correct answer is b.

Test-Taking Hint

You can remember the order of operations using the acronym PEMDAS or you can use a phrase like "Please Excuse My Dear Aunt Sally."

Definitions

terms of an expression: The parts of an expression that are separated by addition or subtraction. For example, in the expression 4c + 2, the terms are 4c and 2.

coefficient: The constant part of a term that also contains a variable. In the term 6x, the coefficient is 6.

like terms: Terms that use exactly the same variables. 2x and 8x are like terms. 4ax and 2x are not like terms.

Like Terms

Terms that have exactly the same variables in an expression can be added and subtracted.

Simplify the expression 6x + 4x.

Step 1: Expressions are simplified by writing them in a simpler form. The Distributive Property lets you simplify algebraic expressions by combining like terms.

$$6x + 4x = (6 + 4)x$$

Step 2: Add inside the parentheses.

$$(6 + 4)x = 10x$$
$$6x + 4x = 10x$$

You can combine like terms by adding or subtracting just the coefficients. $6 + 4 = 10$, so $6x + 4x = 10x$.

Put a small mark next to answers you're not sure of. When you finish your test, go back and check those problems first.

TEST TIME: Show Your Work

Simplify the expression $2(12x - 8x) - x$.

Solution: Use the order of operations to simplify this expression. Do the operations inside the parentheses first.

$$2(12x - 8x) - x$$
$$2(4x) - x$$

There are no exponents, so multiply and divide next.

Multiply a number (2) and an algebraic term ($4x$) by multiplying the numbers and keeping the variables the same.

$$2(4x) - x$$
$$8x - x$$

Finally, add and subtract. The terms left are like terms with a variable of x. When there is a variable by itself, the coefficient is 1, so x is the same as $1x$.

$$8x - x$$
$$7x$$

$$2(12x - 8x) - x = 7x$$

14. Equations

equation: A statement comparing two expressions using an equal sign. The equal sign says that the expressions have the same value.

Write an Equation

Write an equation to model this sentence: A number minus 16 is 22.

Step 1: Choose a variable to represent the unknown number.

$$n = \text{unknown}$$

Step 2: Replace the words with numbers, operation symbols, and variables.

The word *is* means "equals."

A number minus 16 is 22.

$$n - 16 = 22$$

Choose the *equation that best models this situation: Gina worked for seven hours total, some of which were in the garden. The remaining three hours she worked in the barn.*

a. $g - 7 = 3$
b. $7 - g = 3$
c. $3 + 7 = g$
d. $g + 7 = 3$

The sentence in the problem tells you that Gina worked 7 hours. Part of the hours she worked in the garden. This is subtraction. You do not know the number of hours she worked in the garden, so a variable is subtracted. The remaining hours she worked in the barn are 3. This is written as "= 3."

Solution: The correct answer is b.

Test-Taking Hint

Read the questions carefully. Some questions ask for the best answer instead of a correct answer.

Evaluate Equations

Evaluate the equation t ÷ 3 = 10 for t = 33.

Step 1: Evaluating an equation is similar to evaluating an expression. Replace the variable with the value given in the problem.

$$t \div 3 = 10$$
$$33 \div 3 = 10$$

Step 2: Divide. 33 ÷ 3 = 11.

$$11 = 10$$

Step 3: To evaluate an equation, you decide if the values are the same on each side of the equal sign. Compare the left and right sides of the equation. Are they the same? No.

33 is not a solution for $t \div 3 = 10$.

Definition

solution to an equation: The number or set of numbers that makes an equation true.

TEST TIME: Show Your Work

Solve for y.
$3 \times 5 = y$

When you solve an equation, you find the value for the variable that makes the equation true. A true equation is one that has the same value on each side of the equal sign.

When the variable is by itself on one side of the equal sign, you find its value by doing the operations on the other side of the equal sign.

Solution: $3 \times 5 = y$

$15 = y$ or $y = 15$

15. Properties of Equality

Definitions

Addition Property of Equality: When the same value is added to both sides of an equation, the equation is still true.

Subtraction Property of Equality: When the same value is subtracted from both sides of an equation, the equation is still true.

Multiplication Property of Equality: When both sides of an equation are multiplied by the same value, the equation is still true.

Division Property of Equality: When both sides of an equation are divided by the same value, the equation is still true.

Addition Property of Equality

Is the equation 4 + 1 = 5 still true when you add 10 to each side of the original equation?

Step 1: Write the original equation. $\qquad$ $4 + 1 = 5$

Step 2: Add 10 to each side. $\qquad$ $4 + 1 + 10 = 5 + 10$

Step 3: Do the addition. $\qquad$ $15 = 15$

Yes, the equation is still true.

TEST TIME: Explain Your Answer

How can you use the properties of equality to find the value of the expression x − 14 when you know the equation x = 36 is true ?

When an equation is true, it is in balance. One side has the same value as the other. When you change one side of the equation, you must change the other in the same way for it to stay in balance.

Solution: When you know $x = 36$, you can use the Subtraction Property of Equality to find the value of $x - 14$. Subtract 14 from each side of the original equation.

$$x = 36$$
$$x - 14 = 36 - 14$$
$$x - 14 = 22$$

Test-Taking Hint

Be sure to use complete sentences when you are explaining an answer.

Which property is illustrated by the set of equations below?

$$2 + 1 = 3; \ x(2 + 1) = 3x$$

    a. The Associative Property of Multiplication
    b. The Addition Property of Multiplication
    ⓒ The Multiplication Property of Equality
    d. The Distributive Property

The first equation is a simple addition equation. The second equation multiplies each side of the original equation by the variable x. The Multiplication Property of Equality says that you can multiply both sides of an equation by the same value and it will still be true.

Solution: The correct answer is c.

Test-Taking Hint

Remember, if you change one side of an equation, you must change the other side in the same way.

Solving Equations

Use the properties of equality to find the value for x in the equation $x - 1 = 10$.

Step 1: The goal is to get the variable x by itself on one side of the equal sign. You may be able to just look at the equation and say "x is 11." This problem tells you to use the properties of equality to find the value.

Decide what needs to be removed to get the variable x by itself. You need to remove the "$- 1$."

$$x \cancel{- 1} = 10$$

Step 2: Remove the "$- 1$" by doing the opposite, or inverse, operation. In this case, to remove "$- 1$" you need to add 1. When you add 1 to one side of the equation, you must also add it to the other side. Add 1 to each side of the equation.

$$x - 1 + 1 = 10 + 1$$

Step 3: Do the math.

$$x = 11$$

16. Addition Problems

Equations

Solve the equation x + 32 = 86.

Step 1: Decide what needs removed to get the variable *x* by itself. You need to remove the "+ 32."

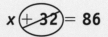

$$x \; \cancel{+\, 32} = 86$$

Step 2: Remove the "+ 32" by doing the opposite, or inverse, operation. In this case, to remove "+ 32" you need to subtract 32. When you subtract 32 from one side of the equation, you must also subtract it from the other side. Subtract 32 from each side of the equation.

$$x + 32 - 32 = 86 - 32$$

Step 3: Do the math.

$$x = 54$$

Test-Taking Hint

Inverse operations can be used to check the answers to computations. For example, use addition to check your subtraction.

TEST TIME: Show Your Work

YoMinh solved the equation
$f + 2 = {}^-6$ *and got the answer* $f = {}^-4.$
Is YoMinh's answer correct? If not, what is the correct answer?

You can check the solution by replacing the variables in an equation with the solution. If the equation is true, the solution is correct.

Solution:
$$f + 2 = {}^-6$$
$${}^-4 + 2 = {}^-6$$
$${}^-2 = {}^-6$$

YoMinh does not have the correct answer.
$$f + 2 = {}^-6$$
$$f + 2 - 2 = {}^-6 - 2$$

The correct answer is $f = {}^-8$

Check the solution.
$$f + 2 = {}^-6$$
$${}^-8 + 2 = {}^-6$$
$${}^-6 = {}^-6$$

Addition Word Problems

A florist pays $12 for a dozen roses, then adds her markup and sells them for $36. Write an algebraic equation and solve it to find the markup on a dozen roses.

Step 1: Write a sentence to show what the problem is saying.

dollars paid plus markup is selling dollars

Step 2: Choose a variable for the value you don't know. Replace the words with numbers, operation symbols, and variables.

Let m = markup
$12 + m = 36$

Step 3: Decide what needs to be removed to get the variable m by itself. You need to remove the 12.

$$\cancel{12} + m = 36$$

Step 4: Remove the 12, or "+ 12"" by doing the opposite, or inverse, operation. Subtract 12 from each side of the equation.

$$12 + m - 12 = 36 - 12$$

Step 5: Do the math.

$$m = 24$$

The markup on a dozen roses is $24.

Test-Taking Hint

Read problems carefully. Decide how you can use the information given to solve the problem.

TEST TIME: Multiple Choice

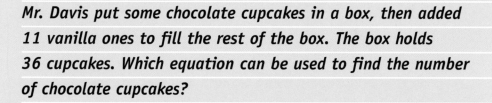

Mr. Davis put some chocolate cupcakes in a box, then added 11 vanilla ones to fill the rest of the box. The box holds 36 cupcakes. Which equation can be used to find the number of chocolate cupcakes?

> a. $c - 11 = 36$
>
> b. $c + 36 = 11$
>
> c. $36 + 11 = c$
>
> (d.) $c + 11 = 36$

Mr. Davis has some cupcakes, then adds some more for a total. This is an addition situation. First, Mr. Davis has some chocolate cupcakes, but the number is unknown. The equation begins with a variable.

Solution: The correct is answer d.

17. Subtraction Problems

Addition and Subtraction

Addition and subtraction are inverse operations. You can sometimes use addition to get a variable by itself in a subtraction problem.

Solve the equation y − 2.5 = 6.3. Check the solution.

Step 1: Decide what needs to be removed to get the variable y by itself. You need to remove the "− 2.5."

$$y \cancel{- 2.5} = 6.3$$

Step 2: Remove the "− 2.5" by doing the opposite, or inverse, operation. Add 2.5 to each side of the equation.

$$y - 2.5 + 2.5 = 6.3 + 2.5$$

Step 3: Do the math.

$$y = 8.8$$

Step 4: Check the solution. Replace the variable in the original problem with the solution.

$$8.8 - 2.5 = 6.3$$
$$6.3 = 6.3$$

TEST TIME: Explain Your Answer

Solve the equation $22 - d = 27$ and explain how you found your solution.

Solution: Add the variable d to both sides of the equation first.

$$22 - d = 27$$
$$22 - d + d = 27 + d$$
$$22 = 27 + d$$

Then subtract 27 from each side to get d by itself.

$$22 = 27 + d$$
$$22 - 27 = 27 + d - 27$$
$$^-5 = d$$

This problem can also be solved by rewriting the subtraction equation as an addition equation. Change the subtraction sign to an addition sign and add the opposite.

$$22 - d = 27$$
$$22 + {}^-d = 27$$

Subtract 22 from each side.

$$22 - 22 + {}^-d = 27 - 22$$
$$^-d = 5$$

If $^-d = 5$, then $d = {}^-5$.

TEST TIME: Show Your Work

Gerald gave the cashier some money to pay for a chili dog, a bag of chips, and a pop. The cashier gave him back $4.75. Write and solve an algebraic equation to find the amount of money Gerald gave the cashier.

Item	Cost
Pizza	$3.00
Hot dog	$2.00
Chili Dog	$2.50
Chips	$1.25
Pop	$1.50
Water	$1.00

One way to write this equation is to use parentheses to add the cost of the items purchased first.
You do not know the amount of money Gerald gave the cashier, so use a variable for that value.

Solution: amount paid minus amount spent equals change

$$p - (\$2.50 + \$1.25 + \$1.50) = \$4.75$$

Add inside the parentheses.

$$p - \$5.25 = \$4.75$$

Solve for p.

$$p - \$5.25 + \$5.25 = \$4.75 + \$5.25$$

$$p = \$10.00$$

Gerald gave the cashier $10.00.

Calculators

Calculators are useful tools for solving and checking the solutions to math problems. It is still important to understand the problem and what to do with the numbers in the problem.

Use a calculator to check the solution to the problem on page 72.

One way: Begin with the solution. Start with $10.00 on the calculator. Subtract the price of each item Gerald purchased.

$$\$10.00 - \$2.50 - \$1.25 - \$1.50 = \$4.75$$

Another way: Begin with the change. Add the price of each item Gerald purchased.

$$\$4.75 + \$2.50 + \$1.25 + \$1.50 = \$10.00$$

18. Multiplication Problems

Coefficients

In an algebraic term that uses multiplication, the number part of the term is called the coefficient. Use division by the coefficient to get the variable by itself.

Solve the equation 7n = 154.

Step 1: Decide what needs to be removed to get the variable *n* by itself. You need to remove the 7.

$$\textcircled{7}n = 154$$

Step 2: Remove the 7 by doing the opposite, or inverse, operation. Divide each side of the equation by the coefficient, 7.

$$\frac{7n}{7} = \frac{154}{7}$$

Step 3: Do the math.

$$n = 22$$

Step 4: Check the solution. Replace the variable in the original problem with the solution.

$$7(22) = 154$$
$$154 = 154$$

TEST TIME: Multiple Choice

Find the value of b.

12b = 132

    a. 8
    b. 10
    c. 13
    (d.) 11

For a problem like this, if you know basic multiplication facts you do not need to use a pencil and paper. In this problem ask yourself what number multiplied with 12 has a product of 132? If you can't do the math in your head, divide both sides by 12 to get *b* by itself.

Solution: The correct is answer d.

Test-Taking Hint

Knowing basic math skills will help you do simple problems quickly and with confidence.

Word Problems

A social committee set up tables for a meeting. Each table seats 8 people. In all, there was seating for 56. How many tables did the committee set up?

Step 1: This problem uses the word *each*. Words such as *each, every, of,* or *per* indicate multiplication. Write a sentence to show what the problem is saying.

number of tables times seats each is total seats

Step 2: Choose a variable for the value you don't know. Replace the words with numbers, operation symbols, and variables.

Let t = number of tables
$$t(8) = 56$$

When a number and variable are multiplied, the number is normally written first.

$$8t = 56$$

Step 3: Decide what needs to be removed to get the variable t by itself. You need to remove the 8. Divide each side of the equation by the coefficient, 8.

$$\frac{8t}{8} = \frac{56}{8}$$

Step 4: Do the math.

$$t = 7$$

The committee set up 7 tables.

Test-Taking Hint

Read word problems carefully. Key words such as "total," "per," "average," or "difference" can help you decide what operation should be performed.

TEST TIME: Explain Your Answer

Taylor said that for the equation
3.79x = 30.32, the solution is x = 6.
Is Taylor correct? Explain how you know.

Solution: No, Taylor is not correct. You can check Taylor's answer using estimation. If you round the decimal numbers to the closest whole number, the equation is close to $4x = 30$.
Test Taylor's solution in the rounded equation. $4 \times 6 = 24$.
24 is too much lower than 30 for 6 to be the correct solution.

19. Division Problems

Variable as the Dividend

Solve the equation $\dfrac{n}{2} = 16$.

Step 1: Decide what needs to be removed to get the variable *n* by itself. You need to remove the 2.

$$\frac{n}{2} = 16$$

Step 2: A fraction bar is often used in algebra to show division. In this equation the variable is the dividend, or number being divided. Remove the 2 by doing the opposite, or inverse, operation. Since the variable is being divided by 2, multiply both sides of the equation by 2.

$$\frac{n}{2}(2) = 16(2)$$

Step 3: Do the math.

$$\frac{n}{2}\left(\frac{2}{1}\right) = 16(2)$$

$$n = 32$$

Step 4: Check the solution. Replace the variable in the original problem with the solution.

$$\frac{32}{2} = 16$$

$$16 = 16$$

TEST TIME: Multiple Choice

Solve y ÷ 4 = 8.

        a. y = 2

        b. y = 16

        (c.) y = 32

        d. y = 64

Some problems can be solved by checking each solution. When you have enough time and don't know how to solve a problem, try putting each solution into the equation.

        a. 2 ÷ 4 = 1/2

        b. 16 ÷ 4 = 4

        c. 32 ÷ 4 = 8

        d. 64 ÷ 4 = 16

Solution: The correct is answer c.

Test-Taking Hint

Most tests are scored on the number of questions you answer correctly, but check first. If you do not lose points for wrong answers, answer every question, even if you have to guess.

Variable as the Divisor

Solve the equation $\dfrac{54}{x} = 6$.

Step 1: Decide what needs to be removed to get the variable x by itself. You need to remove the 54.

$$\frac{54}{x} = 6$$

Step 2: When the variable is the divisor, or number being divided by, it takes two steps to get the variable alone. First, multiply both sides of the equation by x.

$$\frac{54}{x}(x) = 6(x)$$

$$54 = 6x$$

Step 3: Divide each side of the equation by the coefficient, 6.

$$\frac{54}{6} = \frac{6x}{6}$$

$$9 = x \text{ or } x = 9$$

Test-Taking Hint

In some equations, the variable will end on the right side of the equal sign, such as 9 = x. This is a correct solution, but it is better as x = 9. The Symmetric Property in algebra says that if 9 = x, then x = 9.

TEST TIME: Show Your Work

Maddie divided 3.84 pounds of peanuts evenly into containers of trail mix. Each container got 0.48 pounds of peanuts. Write and solve an algebraic equation to find the number of containers.

Solution:

Total divided by number of containers equals amount per container

$$3.84 \div c = 0.48$$

Multiply both sides by c.

$$3.84 \div c \times c = 0.48 \times c$$
$$3.84 = 0.48c$$

Some tests allow you to use calculators.
Use a calculator when you know how to solve a problem,
and it will save you time you may need for other problems.

Use a calculator to divide both sides by 0.48.

$$\frac{3.84}{0.48} = \frac{0.48c}{0.48}$$
$$8 = c$$

Maddie had 8 containers of trail mix.

20. Multi-Step Problems

Two-Step Equations

Algebra problems sometimes have more than one operator. Get the term with the variable by itself first, then get the variable by itself.

Solve $5x - 12 = 3$.

Step 1: Decide what needs to be removed first to get the variable *x* by itself. This equation has two terms on the side with the variable, $5x$ and 12. To get the term with the variable by itself, you need to remove the 12.

$$5x - 12 = 3$$

Step 2: Remove the 12, or "$- 12$" by doing the opposite, or inverse, operation. Add 12 to each side of the equation.

$$5x - 12 + 12 = 3 + 12$$
$$5x = 15$$

Step 3: Divide each side of the equation by the coefficient, 5.

$$\frac{5x}{5} = \frac{15}{5}$$

$$x = 3$$

Step 4: Check the solution.

$$5(3) - 12 = 3$$
$$15 - 12 = 3$$
$$3 = 3$$

TEST TIME: Multiple Choice

What is the first step to solving for n in the equation 4n + 12 = 8?

a. Add 12 to each side.
b. Subtract 12 from each side.
c. Multiply each side by 4.
d. Divide each side by 4

To get the term with the variable by itself, you need to get rid of the "+ 12." Do the opposite operation first. Another way you can think of this is to remove the operations that are farthest away from the variable first.

Solution: The correct is answer b.

TEST TIME: Show Your Work

To find Brenda's average number of putts per hole in miniature golf, she used the equation $9(a - 1) = 45$. What was her average score per hole?

This problem can be solved in two ways. You can distribute the 9 over the subtraction in the parentheses so that the expression on the left is $9a - 9$. Or you can remove the 9 first using division.

Solution:
$$9(a - 1) = 45$$

Divide both sides by a.
$$\frac{9(a - 1)}{9} = \frac{45}{9}$$

$$a - 1 = 5$$

Add 1 to each side.
$$a - 1 + 1 = 5 + 1$$

$$a = 6$$

Brenda averaged 6 putts per hole in miniature golf.

Check the Solution

Is y = 3 a solution for the equation 2(y + 2) − 6 = 4?

Step 1: Check the solution by replacing the variable in the equation with the solution.

$$2(y + 2) - 6 = 4$$
$$2(3 + 2) - 6 = 4$$

Step 2: Do the operations. Remember, when there is more than one operation, use the order of operations. Do the operation inside the parentheses first.

$$2(5) - 6 = 4$$

Do any multiplication and division next.

$$10 - 6 = 4$$

Do any addition and subtraction last.

$$4 = 4$$

Yes, y = 3 is a solution for 2(y + 2) − 6 = 4.

Test-Taking Hint

Word problems should be answered in complete sentences that include units.

21. Inequalities

Inequality Signs

The symbol < means "less than."

The symbol ≤ means "less than or equal to."

The symbol > means "greater than."

The symbol ≥ means "greater than or equal to."

Solution Sets

Use a number line to show the solution set for x ≥ 4.

Step 1: Draw a number line that includes the number 4.

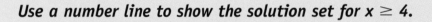

Step 2: Since *x* is greater than or equal to 4, the solution set includes 4. Use a solid circle on the number 4 to show that it is part of the solution set.

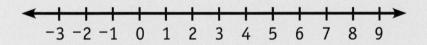

Step 3: Draw a solid line with an arrow over the number line to show all of the numbers greater than 4.

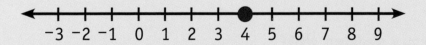

TEST TIME: Multiple Choice

Which inequality is graphed on the number line below?

$$-3 \; -2 \; -1 \; \; 0 \; \; 1 \; \; 2 \; \; 3 \; \; 4 \; \; 5 \; \; 6 \; \; 7 \; \; 8 \; \; 9$$

a. $x \geq 6$

b. $x > 6$

c. $x \leq 6$

d. $x < 6$

An open circle on a number line shows that the number is NOT part of the solution set. Since the line with the arrow is to the left of the number 6, the solution set includes all of the numbers that are less than 6.

Solution: The correct is answer d.

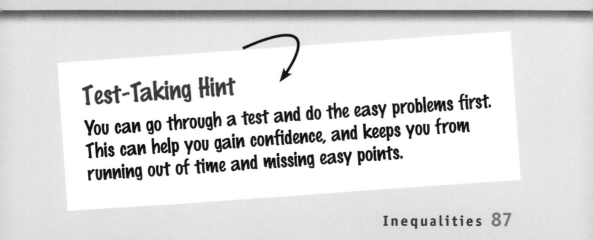

Test-Taking Hint

You can go through a test and do the easy problems first. This can help you gain confidence, and keeps you from running out of time and missing easy points.

Writing an Inequality

To make a profit from a fundraiser, the sophomore class must sell at least 27 raffle tickets. Write an inequality to show the number of raffle tickets the class can sell and earn a profit.

Step 1: Choose a variable to represent the number or numbers you don't know. In this problem, you do not know the number of raffle tickets the sophomore class will sell.

Let r = number of raffle tickets

Step 2: Decide which inequality sign is needed. The problem uses the words *at least*. This means the number of tickets must be equal to 27 or greater than 27.

greater than or equal to: $\geq$

Step 3: Write the inequality.

$$r \geq 27$$

Step 4: Test a value. Choose a value that fits the inequality and see if it makes sense in the problem. The number 30 is greater than 27. If the sophomore class sells 30 raffle tickets, will they make a profit? Yes. The inequality works.

$$r \geq 27$$

TEST TIME: Show Your Work

Abby is 27 years old and her daughter is 3. According to the price chart shown, how much does she need to pay for a one-day pass to the zoo for both her and her daughter?

One-Day Pass	
General Admission	$12.00
Ages <3	$5.00
Ages >65	$10.00

Solution: Abby is 27, so her age does not fit into either of the two discounted rates. She must pay $12.00. Abby's daughter is 3. The discount applies only to children less than 3. Her daughter must also pay the general admission price of $12.00.

$12.00 + $12.00 = $24.00

Abby must pay $24.00 for a one-day pass for her and her daughter.

22. Addition and Subtraction Inequalities

Addition Inequalities

You can add and subtract values from both sides of an inequality in the same way as an equation.

Solve x + 12 > 15.

Step 1: Decide what needs to be removed to get the variable *x* by itself. You need to remove the "+ 12."

$$x + 12 > 15$$

Step 2: Remove the "+ 12" by doing the opposite, or inverse, operation. Subtract 12 from each side of the inequality.

$$x + 12 - 12 > 15 - 12$$

$$x > 3$$

Step 3: Test your answer. Check any number from the solution set. Let's check the number 5.

$$5 + 12 > 15$$
$$17 > 15 \text{ True}$$

Check a number that is not part of the solution set. Let's check 0.

$$0 + 12 > 15$$
$$12 > 15 \text{ Not True}$$

TEST TIME: Multiple Choice

Solve 26.89 + y ≤ 8.42.

     a. $y \leq 18.47$
     ⓑ $y \leq {}^-18.47$
     c. $y \leq 35.31$
     d. $y \leq {}^-35.31$

To get the variable *y* by itself, subtract 26.89 from each side of the inequality. Subtract using either a calculator or a paper and pencil.

$$26.89 - 26.89 + y \leq 8.42 - 26.89$$
$$y \leq {}^-18.47$$

Solution: The correct is answer b.

Test-Taking Hint

Know your calculator. If you're using someone else's calculator, make sure you understand how to use it before you begin a test.

Subtraction Inequalities

Solve and graph the inequality x − 2 < 1.

Step 1: Decide what needs to be removed to get the variable *x* by itself. You need to remove the "− 2." Add 2 to each side of the inequality.

$$x - 2 < 1$$
$$x - 2 + 2 < 1 + 2$$
$$x < 3$$

Step 2: Graph the inequality $x < 3$ on a number line.

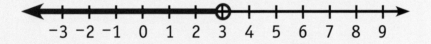

Step 3: Test your answer. Check any number from the solution set. Let's check the number 0.

$$0 - 2 < 1$$
$$^-2 < 1 \text{ True}$$

Check a number that is not part of the solution set. Let's check 3.

$$3 - 2 < 1$$
$$1 < 1 \text{ Not True}$$

TEST TIME: Show Your Work

Casey gave away $20 but still has more than $14. Write and solve an inequality for the amount of money Casey had before he gave some away.

The words *gave away* tell you this is a subtraction situation. The words *more than* tell you to use the greater than sign.

Solution: Total minus amount given away is more than amount left

$$m - \$20 > \$14$$

Add $20 to each side.

$$m - \$20 + \$20 > \$14 + \$20$$

$$m > \$34$$

Casey had more than $34 before he gave some away.

Test-Taking Hint

Check your solutions whenever you can. In word problems, try putting the answer into the problem.

For the problem above, the solution is more than $34. Test $50. If Casey had $50, and gave $20 away, would he still have more than $14? YES!

Multiply or Divide With Positive Numbers

You can multiply and divide positive numbers to solve an inequality in the same way as an equation.

Solve $2n > 6$.

Step 1: Treat the inequality just as an equation. Decide what needs to be removed to get the variable n by itself. You need to remove the 2. Divide each side of the equation by the coefficient, 2.

$$\frac{2n}{2} > \frac{6}{2}$$

$$n > 3$$

Step 2: Test your answer. Check any number from the solution set. Let's check the number 8.

$$2(8) > 6$$
$$16 > 6 \text{ True}$$

Check a number that is not part of the solution set. Let's check 0.

$$2(0) > 6$$
$$0 > 6 \text{ Not true}$$

TEST TIME: Show Your Work

Solve $y \div 10 < 2.6$.

Solution:

$$y \div 10 < 2.6$$

Multiply both sides by 10. $y \div 10 \times 10 < 2.6 \times 10$

$$y < 26$$

Test two values.   Test 20. $y \div 10 < 2.6$

$20 \div 10 < 2.6$

$2 < 2.6$ True

Test 50. $y \div 10 < 2.6$

$50 \div 10 < 2.6$

$5 < 2.6$ Not true

Test-Taking Hint

Multiplication by a power of ten (10, 100, 1000, . . .) moves the decimal point to the right. Division by a power of ten moves the decimal point to the left.

Inequalities and Negative Numbers

Multiplying or dividing both sides of an inequality by a negative number reverses the inequality sign. For example, the less than sign must be changed to the greater than sign.

Multiply both sides of the inequality 3 > 1 by ⁻2. Explain the result.

Step 1: Write the inequality.

$$3 > 1$$

Step 2: Multiply both sides of the inequality by ⁻2. Is the result still true?

$$3(^-2) > 1(^-2)$$
$$^-6 > ^-2$$

The result is not true. To make the new inequality true, reverse the sign.

$$^-6 < ^-2$$

TEST TIME: Multiple Choice

Solve y ÷ ⁻6 ≥ 3.

        a. $y \geq 18$

        b. $y \geq {}^-18$

        c. $y \leq 18$

        (d.)$y \leq {}^-18$

To get the variable *y* by itself, multiply each side of the inequality by ⁻6. Reverse the sign because the number is negative.

$$y \div {}^-6 \geq 3$$
$$y \div {}^-6 \times {}^-6 \leq 3 \times {}^-6$$
$$y \leq {}^-18$$

Solution: The correct is answer d.

Test-Taking Hint

Look at each possible answer closely. These possible answers can be very similar, but only one is correct.

24. Multi-Step Inequalities

Two-Step Inequalities

Inequalities, like equations, sometimes need to be solved in more than one step. Follow the same steps that are used to solve multi-step equations.

Solve 2x − 6 ≥ 4.

Step 1: Decide what needs to be removed first to get the variable *x* by itself. This equation has two terms on the side with the variable, 2*x* and 6. To get the term with the variable by itself, you need to remove the 6.

$$2x - 6 \geq 4$$

Step 2: Remove the 6, or "− 6" by doing the opposite, or inverse, operation. Add 6 to each side of the equation.

$$2x - 6 + 6 \geq 4 + 6$$
$$2x \geq 10$$

Step 3: Divide each side of the equation by the coefficient, 2.

$$\frac{2x}{2} \geq \frac{10}{2}$$

$$x \geq 5$$

Step 4: Test a solution. Let's test 10.

$$2(10) - 6 \geq 4$$
$$20 - 6 \geq 4$$
$$14 \geq 4 \text{ True}$$

TEST TIME: Multiple Choice

What is the first step to solve the
inequality $(x - 6) \div {}^-2 < 9$?

a. Divide by 2, keep the inequality sign.
b. Multiply by -2, reverse the inequality sign.
c. Divide by -2, reverse the inequality sign.
d. Multiply by 2, reverse the inequality sign.

Get the terms inside the parentheses alone first. Since the expression inside the parentheses is being divided by $^-2$, you must multiply by both sides of the inequality by $^-2$ and reverse the inequality sign.

Solution: The correct is answer b.

TEST TIME: Show Your Work

Admission to a county fair is $5.00 and ride tickets are $0.50 each. Use an inequality to find the number of ride tickets David can purchase if he has a total of $20.00 to spend. Does David have enough to buy 20 ride tickets?

Write the inequality first. The unknown is the number of ride tickets. Each ride ticket costs $0.50. David must pay for admission and ride tickets. You know David can spend up to $20.00. This means he can spend less than or equal to $20.00.

Solution:

cost of admission plus cost of ride tickets is less than or equal to total

$$\$5.00 + \$0.50t \le \$20.00$$

Subtract $5.00 from each side.

$$\$5.00 + \$0.50t - \$5.00 \le \$20.00 - \$5.00$$
$$\$0.50t \le \$15.00$$

Divide each side by the coefficient, $0.50.

$$\frac{\$0.50t}{\$0.50} \le \frac{\$15.00}{\$0.50}$$
$$t \le 30$$

TEST TIME: Continued

Test a value that is a solution. Test 10.

$$\$5.00 + \$0.50(10) \le \$20.00$$
$$\$5.00 + \$5.00 \le \$20.00$$
$$\$10.00 \le \$20.00 \text{ True}$$

Test a value that is not a solution. Test 100.

$$\$5.00 + \$0.50(100) \le \$20.00$$
$$\$5.00 + \$50.00 \le \$20.00$$
$$\$55.00 \le \$20.00 \text{ Not true}$$

To answer the second part of the question:

Twenty tickets is less than 30 tickets, so yes, David has enough to buy 20 ride tickets.

Test-Taking Hint

Make sure you answer the question that is asked. Some problems require more than one step. In this problem, you must write an inequality, solve it, then decide if David has enough to buy 20 ride tickets.

Further Reading

Books

McKellar, Danica. *Math Doesn't Suck: How to Survive Middle School Math Without Losing Your Mind or Breaking a Nail.* New York: Hudson Street Press, 2007.

Miller, Robert. *Bob Miller's Algebra for the Clueless.* New York: McGraw-Hill, 2007.

Rozakis, Laurie. *Get Test Smart!: The Ultimate Guide to Middle School Standardized Tests.* New York: Scholastic Reference, 2007.

Internet Addresses

Banfill, J. *AAA Math.* 2009.
<http://www.aaastudy.com/alg.htm>

MathsIsFun.com. *Algebra.* 2007.
<http://www.mathsisfun.com/algebra/definitions.html>
<http://www.mathsisfun.com/algebra/index.html>

Testtakingtips.com. *Test Taking Tips.* 2003–2010.
<http://www.testtakingtips.com/test/math.htm>

Index

Index